CCSS **Genre** Expository Text

MW00474851

Essential Question
How do we use energy?

WIND POWER

by Ann Weil

CHAPTER 1 | WHAT IS WIND?

Have you ever been outside on a windy day? What did the wind feel like? Could you feel it push against you as you walked? The wind can blow a leaf off a tree, keep a kite in the sky, or even push a sailboat.

For thousands of years, people have used wind power to sail across rivers and seas. People had sailboats in ancient Egypt. They sailed up and down the Nile River. They would load their sailboats with goods and carry them down the river. Later, people set sail from Europe. They sailed across the oceans. They discovered new places, including the Americas. Some people even used sailboats to travel around the world.

The mainsail captures wind energy to move the sailboat.

Energy from the Sun warms the air over land more quickly than the air over water.

Just what is wind, anyway? Wind is moving air. The wind can be breezy and calm. It can also be very powerful, causing damage to our homes.

Wind has **kinetic energy**, the force that moves things. Wind gets this energy from the Sun. First the Sun's heat warms the air. Warm air, which is lighter than cool air, rises up. Then cooler air takes its place. This moving air is the wind.

CHAPTER 2 | WINDMILLS

Sailboats were not the only way that people used wind power long ago. They also built windmills. Windmills help capture energy from the wind. They make it possible for us to use wind power to do work.

Let's take a closer look at windmills. They have long arms. These arms move in a circle when the wind blows on them. The turning arms provide power for machines inside the windmill.

This windmill was built in 1902 to pump water in Golden Gate Park in San Francisco, California.

The History of Windmills

People can use windmills to pump water. In the 1800s and 1900s, Americans built windmills for this purpose. Many people had ranches and farms in dry places. They couldn't just haul buckets of water from rivers. Instead, people used windmills to pump water up from deep underground. Then they could use the water for drinking, cooking, watering crops, and feeding farm animals.

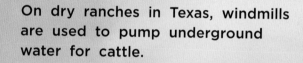

On dry ranches in Texas, windmills are used to pump underground water for cattle.

This use of windmills is nothing new. People in China used simple windmills more than 2,000 years ago. They mainly used them to pump water. People in Persia (modern-day Iran) used windmills around 650 CE. These early windmills had sails. People used them to grind grain to make food. People in the Middle East used windmills this way, too. By the 1100s, people in Europe also used windmills. Around this time, someone found a way to make windmills work even better.

This windmill in Greece is from the 1500s.

Early windmills turned on a horizontal, or side-to-side, axis. But they could make more power when the arms turned on a vertical, or up-and-down, axis. This discovery made a big difference! Soon it led to the design of a new kind of windmill, which was used in Holland.

The new Dutch windmills had four long arms. Each arm had a sail or wooden slat. People used these windmills to pump water, too. But instead of pumping it up for people to use, they pumped it away from the land. The windmills drained marshes and lakes near the sea. This gave the people more land for farms.

The Dutch also built walls, or dikes, to hold back the sea.

CHAPTER 3
WINDMILLS TO WIND FARMS

People still use windmills to pump water. And now we also use wind power to make electricity. Electricity is a kind of energy, or power. Most of us use some form of it every day. Look around your home or school. Do you see electric plugs in the wall? Energy flows through to provide power.

Refrigerators, computers, and other appliances use electricity.

Clean Energy
Power companies make electricity in different ways. One way is to burn **fossil fuels**, such as coal or oil. But burning fossil fuels causes pollution. Wind power does not pollute the air or water.

Wind Turbines

Modern windmills used to generate electricity are called wind **turbines**. The first wind turbines were used in Denmark around 1890. Some places in the United States began using wind turbines in the early 1900s.

Wind turbines come in different sizes. A small one can produce enough electricity for a home or a school. A large one can produce enough for a small community. One huge wind turbine in Vermont in the 1940s produced enough electricity for a small town.

Some people use small turbines to provide energy for their homes.

Did You Know?
Most of the wind turbines in the United States are in California.

9

A wind farm is a group of turbines that are connected together. Linking these turbines helps them work better. Wind farms work best in places that have strong, steady winds. Turbines usually have two or three blades. The blades are made in a special shape to catch the wind. The blades on a wind turbine can spin as fast as 200 miles per hour!

Some wind farms are on land. Some are **offshore**. Wind farms on land and out at sea can make a lot of electricity. Exactly how much they produce depends on the size of the turbine and the wind speed.

This wind farm at Altamont Pass in California is one of the oldest in the United States.

Small turbines work well. But large turbines with large blades produce more energy at a lower cost than smaller turbines. So most wind farms use large turbines with a lot of space in between each one. Some large turbines are 20 stories high. Their blades stretch out over an area larger than a football field.

One of the largest wind turbines is in Germany and stands 453 feet (138 meters) tall.

Tall Turbines
The average height of a small wind turbine is 200 feet. That's about twice as tall as a regular telephone pole.

CHAPTER 4
THE FUTURE OF WIND POWER

Some people like using wind power because it is a clean way to make electricity. It does not pollute the air or water. Other people do not like wind farms. Wind farms can be noisy. The turbines' whirring blades also make the ground shake. People thousands of feet away from wind farms complain about the problems they cause. Wind farms may sometimes harm animals, too. Bats and birds may fly into the spinning blades.

These are serious problems. So, experts are working on ways to make wind farms better. They have found new ways to make turbines quieter. Wind power may never be silent. But building wind farms offshore and far away from people can help. That way, people are less bothered by the noise. Experts are also looking for ways to keep bats and birds safe.

Birds are more likely to be harmed flying into buildings than into wind farms.

Power plants that burn coal pollute the air.

Finding good sources of energy is important. Right now, the United States buys oil from other countries to meet our country's huge demand for energy. This costs a lot of money. The cost affects all Americans. But there is plenty of wind right here at home!

Wind power may be the answer to the world's growing need for electricity. It costs less than other ways to make electricity. One day we will run out of oil, coal, and other fossil fuels. But we will never run out of wind!

Respond to Reading

Summarize

Use important details to summarize *Wind Power*.

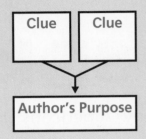

Text Evidence

1. How do you know *Wind Power* is expository text? GENRE

2. Why do you think the author wrote this selection? AUTHOR'S PURPOSE

3. Use paragraph clues to figure out the meaning of the word *kinetic* on page 3. PARAGRAPH CLUES

4. Write about what you have learned about wind power from this selection. WRITE ABOUT READING

Compare Texts
Read about how people use a different form of energy.

A S☀lar House

Many Americans live in places with very cold winters. How should they heat their homes? Which energy source is the best?

Some people have furnaces that burn oil. Some have stoves that burn wood or wood pellets. Some use electric heaters to stay warm. Today, many people are using solar energy to heat their homes. They use special equipment to make their own electricity instead of buying it from a power company.

SOLAR ENERGY

Look at rooftops in your neighborhood. You might see solar panels on some roofs. Solar panels change heat and light energy from the Sun into electricity. But you can use the Sun's energy to heat your home even if it does not have solar panels. Some homes use **passive solar** heating. The home is built to help move heat from sunny rooms to other rooms that get less sun.

This home uses solar heating during cold weather.

solar panels

back-up heater

Solar panels capture the Sun's energy and turn it into heat.

Make Connections

What are wind and solar energy used for?

ESSENTIAL QUESTION

How is energy collected in *Wind Power* and *A Solar House*? TEXT TO TEXT

Glossary

fossil fuels *(FOS-uhl FYEW-uhlz)* energy sources, such as coal and oil, that come from fossils *(page 8)*

kinetic energy *(ki–NET-ik EN-ur-jee)* energy that is caused by movement *(page 3)*

offshore *(of-SHAWR)* in the sea some distance from the shore *(page 10)*

passive solar *(PAS-iv SOH-lur)* a type of heating that uses solar energy without depending on machines *(page 17)*

turbines *(TUR-bighnz)* an engine with blades that spin to create power *(page 9)*

Index

Focus
on
Science

Purpose To make a wind sock

What to Do

Step 1 ► You will need the following: two pieces of thick paper, tape, and string. Roll one piece of paper into a tube and tape it shut.

Step 2 ► Cut the other piece of paper into strips and tape the strips to the bottom of the tube. Tape string across the top of the tube.

Step 3 ► Tie the string on the windsock to an object outside. Choose a windy place far away from buildings and trees.

Conclusion Summarize what happened when wind blew on the windsock. Draw a labeled diagram that explains your results.